# Legends of Country Music

# Garth Brooks

## An unauthorized fan tribute

## By: James Hoag

**Paperback Edition**

Manufactured in the United States of America

# CONTENTS

# INTRODUCTION

About a year or so ago, my wife and I travelled to Las Vegas to the Wynn Casino to see Garth Brooks perform. Now, I had heard stories about his concerts but had never had the good fortune to actually see one. I was really looking forward to this night.

We entered the concert hall and took our seats. There was a lone stool on stage. Nothing else. Just the stool.

I thought, *'What the heck?'*

We waited and soon Garth walked out, sat on the stool, and began to talk to the audience and sing songs that had influenced him when he was first getting into the music business.

I thought, *'OK, this is cool but where is the band? Where is the Garth that runs around the stage and flies above the audience and yells and screams?'*

I thought, *'I know, this is just the first half. After the intermission, he'll do the rowdy stuff.'*

But, he never did. The show you see at the Wynn is just Garth, sitting on the stool, and playing the guitar. But somewhere about 30 minutes into the concert, I realized I was seeing magic. I was seeing the real Garth Brooks, not the stuntman, but a true performer who loves the music he sings.

He takes you on a journey through the history of music as it influenced him. He talks about the two Gods of Country Music: Haggard and Jones. Yes, he did sing his hits and a lot more besides. At one point in the performance, he brought out Trisha Yearwood, his wife, and they sang a couple of duets. It was magical.

I was in awe. I thought, this isn't the Garth I thought I would see, but it's the Garth that everyone should see. I walked out of the Wynn in a haze.

I told my wife, "I think we just saw the best concert we have ever seen."

And, I'm not a young man. I've seen lots of concerts. Garth could not have done a better job.

This series of books is called Legends of Country Music, and I'm not sure some people would not consider Garth Brooks a legend. After all, he had his first hit in 1989. Has enough time passed for him to be considered a legend? I think so. Garth Brooks is, by far, my favorite country singer, and I like almost all country singers. I was crushed, in 2000, when he announced he was "retiring." And, I was ecstatic when it was announced that he was coming to the Wynn. I knew I had to see it. I'm so glad I did.

# "LET'S START AT THE BEGINNING..."

"Let's start at the beginning..." (Garth Brooks at the beginning of his Wynn concert.) Garth Brooks was born Troyal Garth Brooks on February 7, 1962 at St. John Medical Center in Tulsa, Oklahoma to parents Troyal Raymond Brooks (everyone called him 'Raymond") and Colleen Carroll. To quote Garth, "My mother was a pistol, and my dad was in charge." Raymond was an engineer and draftsman with Union Oil. For Colleen and Raymond, this was a second marriage for both of them. Colleen came into the marriage with three children: Jim, Jerry, and Betsy. Raymond had one son from a previous marriage. So, right from the beginning, the home was filled with children. The two had another son, named Kelly, born in 1960. Eighteen months later, Garth joined the family and now they were complete. Garth was now the youngest of six children.

Living in Tulsa was a hassle so in 1966, they moved to Yukon, Oklahoma, a small town about fifteen miles southwest of Oklahoma City. Yukon only had about 21,000 people in 2010, so it must have been about half that size back in the mid-Sixties. If you want to grow up and be a musician, you have to start early. Garth was showing his talent when he as young as two. He would sing and perform for the family every chance he got. He was a born "ham." He loved being in the spotlight. As a boy, he loved sports but was really not very good at them. He especially liked baseball and played for the local school team.

This was the Seventies when Garth did most of his growing up. The music of the day was James Taylor and Elton John. Garth loved rock and roll but he also loved the country music his father played on the home phonograph. Garth says during his Wynn concert that the God his father worshiped was "Haggard and Jones." As he said that, he would place one arm vertical at the mention of Haggard and the other arm horizontal when saying Jones in the shape of a cross. This was the religion of the family.

Garth got hold of a guitar when he was in ninth grade and started practicing. It was only a three-string, but he managed. He upgraded it as soon as he could. When he was sixteen, someone gave him a banjo, and he learned to play that as well. He became interested in bluegrass and started several bands with his classmates to perfect his art. None of the other boys ever stayed with the band for very long, but Garth knew what he wanted to do. This was his future.

Garth was interested in pretty much just two things (besides girls; that is.) He liked sports, and he liked music. He wasn't that good at sports, so his future had to lie in music. He graduated from High School in 1980 and while he wasn't good enough at sports to make a career out of it, he was good enough to get a track scholarship to Oklahoma State University in Stillwater, Oklahoma. There, he participated in track by throwing the javelin. He was a member of the Alpha Gamma Rho fraternity which is an agricultural fraternity. Garth did not exactly come from a farming background, but I assume he fit in just fine with the other guys.

It was in 1981 that Garth heard the song that would change his life. George Strait, who we know went on to become a country superstar in his own right, recorded his first record in 1980. "Unwound" was Strait's first record and his first hit, reaching number six on the Country charts. Garth heard the song on the car radio, and it hit him like a ton of bricks. He knew that was what he wanted to do. If you're smart, you don't go into the music business without a backup plan. Garth knew the odds were against him if he just started playing music, so it was wise of him to stay in school and get a degree. That way, he would have something to fall back on if he couldn't make a living playing music.

Part of the time Garth went to college, he roomed with his brother Kelly, who was older than him. When Kelly graduated, Garth needed a new roommate and got together with Ty England. This is worth mentioning because England went on to sing country music as well but didn't have the career that Garth did. He joined Garth's band during the early years and then went on his own around 1995.

Garth graduated from Oklahoma State in 1984 with a degree in advertising. He never really used his education, however, because almost as soon as he graduated he went on the road with his band, playing at small clubs and bars. Garth had formed several different bands during his college years but was now playing solo. He would come on stage at Willie's saloon in Stillwater wearing sweatpants and a white T-shirt and a baseball cap and everyone would pay attention. They had heard about this new singer and knew just how good he was.

Garth could sing just about anything. He didn't have any of his own music yet, but he played all the classics, country and rock included. He sang James Taylor and Styx and George Strait all back to back. The crowd loved it. He was paid $100 for a four hour set. This was good money back in the early eighties, but he didn't work regularly. He soon found out that a given club could only use him for a few nights and then he had to move on to somewhere else. The work was good when he had work, but he wasn't making a living, so he took a part time job working at a sports equipment store right near the clubs he worked at night.

Finding he still needed money, he also worked as a bouncer at a tavern in Stillwater. Some of this was during school and some of it was after he graduated. It was while working as a bouncer, that he developed a real dislike for alcohol. The smell coming out of the bar was strong, and it made him sick. Garth was never much of a drinker after that.

This reminds me of a story in my own life. When I was about 16, I was babysitting for a friend, and she had some cigarettes lying in the open that she had forgotten about.

I thought, *'Everyone who is cool smokes. I'm going to try it, too.'*

But having never smoked a cigarette before, when I tried to inhale the smoke, I swallowed it instead of breathing it in. The smoke in my stomach made me so sick, I almost threw up. For the next week, every time I got near someone who was smoking, my stomach would roll over and I would come close to being sick again. After that first time, I was never tempted to smoke again.

The bar where Garth worked as a bouncer was called The Tumbleweed Ballroom. It was here that he met Sandy Mahl.

# SANDY MAHL

Sandy Mahl, who would become Garth's first wife and mother of his three daughters, was born in 1965 in the same hospital that Garth was born in three years earlier. Her parents were John and Pat Mahl, and she grew up in rural Yukon, Oklahoma, just like Garth did. She had one older sister named Debbie, and the two were expected to pull their weight around the house. This was a fine, typical, American home in which to grow up. She went to school like everyone else, did her chores at night when she got home, and went to college when she graduated from high school. She had always promised her mother that she would go to college and in 1983, she delivered on that promise, attending Oklahoma State University.

It was during her freshman year that she met Garth Brooks. The way they met is interesting. While he was working as a bouncer at the Tumbleweed, Sandy and a friend decided to stop by. In the Ladies Room, the friend, having had too much to drink, got into an argument with Sandy. Sandy, also probably having had too much to drink, decided to settle the argument by taking a swing at her friend. She missed and hit the wall instead, imbedding her hand in the wall. She found she could not remove it and so they called Garth in to help.

He helped her get free and since Sandy was in no shape to drive home, Garth, the gentlemen that he was, offered to drive her home. She would have to wait until his shift was over, but that was OK. Sandy liked what she saw and so did Garth. In the car, they got to know each other.

After college, in 1985, Garth decided to travel to Nashville, the home of Country music, and see what he could see. It was a twelve-hour drive. He half expected to be welcomed with open arms, everybody just waiting to throw a contract at him and get him started in the music business. We all know it doesn't work that way. He did have an appointment with Merlin Littlefield, the director of ASCAP in Nashville. Most of the thousands of artists that came to the Music City did not even have that. Littlefield politely listened to Garth's demo tape and then, as gently as he could, told him to go home. The most discouraging moment of the trip was when a famous song writer that Garth had heard of, someone whose music he knew, came into Littlefield's office and asked for a $500 loan to help pay his bills.

Garth was crushed. This was a rude awakening, and Garth decided maybe he wasn't ready for Nashville, so he put his tail between his legs and turned the car back toward Oklahoma and went home to figure out what, if anything, he should do next. His mother, Colleen, was sympathetic. She knew the business and knew just how hard it could be. She consoled him as best she could and knew that Garth would try again.

So, he went back to doing what he had done before. He played the local bars; he renewed his relationship with Sandy (she was a little upset that he had gone to Nashville without telling her); he wrote new music.

He organized a band with several of his friends that he called Santa Fe. The friends were Jed Lindsay on lead guitar, Tom Skinner on bass, and Matt O'Meilia on drums. It took a little convincing, but the others were soon on board. They went to work at Bink's, a new club in Stillwater. For their little band, this was as big as it got in Stillwater. This is where Garth would develop the style of playing and singing that would follow him the rest of his career. They played mostly cover songs but did decide to include one new song. This was one of the first songs that Garth had written. Up until now, no one had heard the song, but the customers at Bink's liked it. The song: "Much Too Young (To Feel This Damn Old)."

"Much Too Young" was basically a tribute to worn out cowboys that ride the circuit, especially Chris LeDoux. On his twelve hour ride to Nashville and back, Garth had played a tape of LeDoux's music over and over. Chris LeDoux had always been an idol of sorts to Garth, and he wanted to honor him in this song. Later, when the song was released and became Garth's first hit, LeDoux heard his name when the radio played the song. He called up Garth and the two were friends from then on. Garth always uses every opportunity he can to honor LeDoux.

But that was still in the future. For now, they had to be satisfied playing for the crowd at Bink's. Garth convinced Tom Skinner's brother, Mike, to join the group as a fiddle player. Now they were five; just the right number for a country band.

On May 24, 1986, they took the night off, and Garth and Sandy were married with smiling members of each family all there. There was no time for a honeymoon, not if you want to make great things happen, so Garth and Santa Fe went back to work, and he and Sandy moved into a small home in Stillwater to begin their lives together.

Santa Fe kept working and kept improving. They played every chance they got. They even went to New Mexico and played in front of complete strangers. They loved it. Garth knew they could make it big in the business. It just took the right circumstances and the right breaks.

# GOING BACK TO NASHVILLE

In early 1987, Garth started making preparations to return to Nashville. This time he wasn't alone: he had his band, Santa Fe with him. All the members of the band were willing to travel to Nashville except one, Matt O'Meilia, who had just finished college and wanted to be a high school teacher, so they had to get a new drummer. They found him in Troy Jones, a local guy who had had a lot of experience playing with country bands around the area. They played their last show in Oklahoma in May of 1987.

Moving to Nashville was an adventure. No one really knew if they had what it took to make it in Nashville. The city was not kind to the thousands of musicians that came there every year looking for the golden ring. So, here came Garth and his entourage. There were five musicians, two wives, one child, and a dog. The dog belonged to Garth and Sandy and was a Siberian Huskie named Sasha.

They say it's not what you know but who you know. It doesn't always make any difference how talented you are. You need persistence and luck to make it in this business, and Garth had both. Garth knew a songwriter from Stillwater named Bob Childers. Childers now lived in Nashville and had had some success with his songs and now had four albums to his credit. Childers knew another songwriter in Nashville named Stephanie Brown who had created two publishing companies. Childers took Garth to see Brown.

Stephanie Brown was willing to listen and asked to hear some of Garth's work. He handed her a cassette tape of some songs that he had recorded and Brown was "blown away" by what she heard. She knew Garth could become a huge star, and she called him up and told him so. She introduced Garth to Bob Doyle, an executive at ASCAP. I suspect that Garth was a little hesitant to meet another ASCAP executive, considering the experience he'd had back in 1985, but Doyle treated him entirely different. Doyle recognized his talent right away.

1987 and 1988 were spent writing songs and playing when and where they could. A lot of the songs written during this period were co-written with other people: writers like Kent Blazy, Pat Alger, and Larry Bastian. It was Blazy who introduced Garth to a new up and coming young singer who was waiting for her first break named Trisha Yearwood. Yearwood would later have a profound effect on the life of Garth Brooks.

These were discouraging years for the Brooks family. Sometimes things move slowly in the music business. Garth and his band were working but not a lot. He held down three jobs and Sandy also worked just to put food on the table. They thought about going back to Oklahoma, but Garth had done that once already. This time, he was in it for keeps. It was do or die. There was no turning back. The rest of the band was not so committed. They all went back to Oklahoma while Garth stayed in Nashville.

They say it takes a village to raise a child. Well, it also takes quite a crowd of people to create a superstar. Garth gradually built up a team of people who could help him get to where he wanted to go. Bob Doyle was ready to leave ASCAP and create his own publishing company. So Major Bob Music came into existence and one of the first songwriters he hired was Garth. Doyle also organized a management company with Pam Lewis, a Nashville publicist. They signed Garth as their first client. Joe Harris, a booking agent, was working in Nashville at the time and got to know Garth. Harris heard Garth sing and immediately was converted. He said at the time that Garth would be "as big as Elvis." Slowly, the team was emerging.

A local "listening room" named The Bluebird Café was run by a woman named Amy Kurland. The Bluebird is still there today, but in

1988, an unknown Garth Brooks came there to play and learn how to perform in front of a Nashville audience. If you look at their website, they brag to this day that Garth played there before he became famous.

One night while he was playing the Bluebird, the forces of fate came together and Garth found himself singing in front of Lynn Shults who was a buyer for Capitol Records. Now, Capitol had initially rejected Garth when he sent them a demo tape but now that Shults saw him perform in public, how he held the crowd and how he interacted with them, he was sold. He called Capitol and told them, "Remember the guy we passed on, Garth Brooks? I think we should take a second look."

Shortly thereafter, Garth had a record contract. Capitol paid him $10,000 to go into the studio and record four singles. Now, in order to go further, he needed a producer. That came from Pam Lewis who knew a guy named Allen Reynolds. Reynolds had been working in Nashville since 1970 and had handled many famous names. He and Garth became friends almost immediately.

Thus, the recording began. They needed four songs to fulfill the Capitol contract. That should be easy. Garth had many he had written from which to choose. He assembled a studio band and then started to think about a road band, which usually was not the same personnel as the studio band. He remembered his promise to bring in his friends from Stillwater, so he called them one by one to ask if they'd like to come back to Nashville to go on tour with him.

They all had one excuse or another and, as it turned out, only two were willing to leave their life for an uncertain future. One was Ty England. I think we can assume England was glad he made the jump since he became a star on his own a few years later. The other was David Gant, who had been a member of one of the many bands Garth had created during his years at college.

The road band was shaping up nicely. They hired several new musicians to play, including James Garver on guitar, Steve McClure on petal steel and electric guitar, Mike Powers on drums, and Tom Bowers on bass. Bowers also acted as their road manager. This was a new band, so it needed a new name. Santa Fe was gone; therefore, Garth decided to name the band after his college town, so he called it Stillwater.

Once the four singles were complete, they played them for the executives at Capitol Records and they said, "Let's make an album."

# THE FIRST ALBUM

The first album to come out of Capitol was the self-titled *Garth Brooks*. The album was released on April 12, 1989, but about a month before that, in March, they released the first single from the album. A single is almost always released prior to the album to generate buzz and interest and to increase sales when the album does finally hit the stores. The first single was, of course, "Much Too Young (To Feel This Damn Old)."

Everybody thinks that Garth Brooks was an overnight sensation. It didn't quite work that way. "Much Too Young" did not exactly take the world by storm. Garth and his crew had to travel around to various radio stations to ask them to play it. No one knew who this Brooks guy was and no one knew just how good the song was. "Much Too Young" peaked at number eight on the Billboard Country Charts which was a pretty good showing for a debut single.

The album did very well for a first album, peaking at number thirteen on the overall Billboard Hot 200 album chart and number two on the Country album chart. This is a fairly short album, only about 32 minutes in length. There are just ten songs which was the standard in the late Eighties and even up until today. Garth says that when he listens to it today, it seems very innocent and he remembers the fear he had when it first came out. Who knew if it would be a success? They had done everything they could to make it a success; now it was up to the public.

The public didn't let them down. The album did well, so they released a second single. "If Tomorrow Never Comes," co-written by Garth and Blazy, was released in August of 1989 and debuted on the country charts on September 9. It quickly went to number one on December 9 and stayed on the charts for a total of 26 weeks. "If Tomorrow Never

Comes" would go on to become, probably, Garth's most recognized song of his career. It became a kind of "signature song" for him and has been covered by many other artists.

The song was awarded the Favorite Country Single at the *American Music Awards* for 1989. Garth was nominated for Top New Male Vocalist of the Year at the *1989 Academy of Country Music Awards* but lost to Clint Black. "If Tomorrow Never Comes" was nominated for Song of the Year and Single Record of the Year at the same *ACM Awards*, but he lost both of them. Things would be much better the next year.

This was his first love song but, of course, not his last. The words of the song really struck home to me the first time I heard it. In the song, the man sings of his love for his wife sleeping next to him. If he were to die during the night, would she know just how much he loved her? At the time, I was having marital problems and I wondered if the reason I was having the problems was that I didn't tell her I loved her enough. I suspect most men go through this at some point in their lives.

"If Tomorrow Never Comes" was also Garth's first video. Garth worked well in front of a camera. He seemed very relaxed and easy with the shot. However, when he saw the finished product, he cried. It seems that some of the shots reminded him of times he had spent with Sandy and things were not well in the Brooks house at this time. Sandy had found out that Garth was cheating on her when he was on the road with his band. She had threatened to leave him.

During a concert, he was in the middle of a song when he broke down, right in front of the audience. He stopped the show, stood at the microphone, and told the crowd what was going on in his life. He then regained his composure and finished the song, after which the crowd gave him a standing ovation. He heard a voice in the back of the group yell out, "Go home to her, Garth." So he did, and he and Sandy worked on the marriage and fixed it, and he promised never to cheat again and then they went back to normal. This problem would rear its ugly head again in a few years but for now, everything was good.

This is the song that cemented my love of Garth Brooks. His first hit "Much Too Young" was a cool song, but it was like a lot of other country songs. "If Tomorrow Never Comes" was something truly different and truly special. I knew that Garth Brooks would become a power in country music.

Garth and Stillwater spent the last half of 1989 touring. They were a success everywhere they went. I once saw a George Strait concert. George pretty much just stands there and sings. It's great, don't get me wrong, but there's not a lot of theatrics in the show. The same is true of Alan Jackson, arguably one of the best country singers of our time, but he just stands and sings. It's wonderful, but, like George Strait, not a lot of theatrics. Garth put on a show. He ran around the stage and threw his hat into the audience and established the high energy shows that he would later become famous for. Everyone who saw Garth and his band would remember him. He didn't seem like a performer. He seemed like a friend. When you were in audience, you felt like he was singing right to you.

The next song released from the album was "Not Counting You." This hit the charts in January of 1990 and "only" peaked at number two. I tried to find the song that kept it out of number one and I believe it was "Hard Rock Bottom of Your Heart" by Randy Travis, but I can't be sure. It did reach number one in Canada. Remember the four songs that Capitol required to see what they could do? "Not Counting You" was the first one recorded of the four, so this is Garth's first recorded song even though it was released third.

There was yet one more song to be released from that first album. "The Dance," written by Tony Arata, was released in April of 1990, hit the charts on May 5th, and went right to number one where it would stay for three weeks. This may well be Garth's signature song. (OK, you can have more than one signature song.) Garth says the meaning of the song is two-fold: one, it is a love song that describes the end of a passionate love affair and two, it is talking about someone who had died because of something he believed in. The video shows several people who have died while engaged in something they believed in. Martin Luther King is shown, as is President John F Kennedy, as well as lesser know people like Keith Whitley, a country singer who died from alcohol poisoning.

Remember the Bluebird Café? Garth was there one night as a customer when he heard the guy who wrote the song, Tony Arata, sing it from the stage. He thought to himself, '*If I ever get an album, that song will be on it.*' And so it is.

During the annual Fan Fair in Nashville, Garth played for his fans. In the middle of one of those concerts, Jimmy Bowen, the president of Capitol Records, came on stage and presented Garth with his Gold Record for selling 500,000 copies. It had only been a couple months, and he was well on his way.

# "Friends in Low Places"

Garth's second album *No Fences* was released on August 27, 1990 and this one did go to number one on the Country charts. It also reached number three on the Billboard Hot 200 which includes all genres. It stayed in the top 40 of the Hot 200 for 126 weeks, which, if you're good at math was about 2 and a half years. As popular as his other albums were, *No Fences* is his biggest selling album with total sales of over $17 Million.

The album contains four of Garth's biggest hits, starting with "Friends in Low Places" which spent four weeks at number one. While Garth was becoming a well-known name among the fans of country music, I think this is the song that really put him into superstar status. Written by DeWayne Blackwell and Earl "Bud" Lee, this is a fun song. A lot of country songs start out in bars, and this one is no exception. The idea for the song came when DeWayne and Bud were out drinking one night and when it came time to pay the tab, Dewayne asked Bud how he was going to pay for it. Bud said, "Don't worry; I've got friends in low places." That was the seed that germinated into a great song.

When I think back on the Nineties, I think of this as Garth's first song, even though he had had several hits before it. "Friends in Low Places" really put him over the top. The rest of the world seemed to agree with me as it won the 1991 Single of the Year at both the *Country Music Association (CMA) Awards* and the *Academy of Country Music (ACM) Awards* that year.

Garth had actually recorded a demo of the song way back before his first album *Garth Brooks* came out, but that album was full, so he couldn't include it. When work was being done on *No Fences*, he contacted the writers and asked if the song was still available. It was, so Garth included it. In the meantime, Mark Chesnutt also recorded the song for his album *Cold At Home*. I just listened to Chesnutt's version on YouTube, and while it's obvious it's the same song, Chesnutt's version is much more subdued than Garth's. Garth really picks up the tempo on the chorus, and I think that makes all the different.

Also, listen to the Garth version, toward the end, the song turns into a real party has you can hear many voices in the background singing along with Garth. They brought 50 people into the studio when they taped the song and they all joined in. Beer was provided for the event, so the people really are having a party. It is said that if you listen closely enough, you can hear the pop of the top of a beer can. I have listened to the song several times and don't hear it, but you might. Give it a try.

The song was such a hit that Garth received letters from high school seniors all over the country wanting to make the song their "class song." These letters were soon followed by other letters from high school principals opposing using the song because it glorified drinking (one of the mainstays of country music.) Garth agreed with the principals. He said that while they had a fun time recording the song and he enjoyed it, it was not the kind of song to base your values on. So, the students were denied use of the song.

The original song only had two verses. In 1991, while he was singing the song live, Garth added a third verse. The words of the third verse are: "Just wait 'til I finish this glass / Then sweet little lady, I'll head back to the bar / And you can kiss my ass." The first time I heard this, I was listening to a live performance and I think it took the crowd by surprise as the noise in the audience rises considerably when he says "You can kiss by ass." It certainly took me by surprise since I had never heard it before that day. It is pure Garth Brooks and pure country.

In the summer of 1990, Garth played a concert at Forest Park in New York City. Forest Park is relatively small, nothing like Central Park, and only holds about 2000 people. On the day that Garth showed up, it was hot (this was August) and over 12,000 people showed up to see him. This is remarkable because this was country and it was New York, not two things you would usually put together, but Garth had fans everywhere. The people loved him.

# GRAND OLE OPRY

On October 6, 1990, Garth was asked to become a member of the Grand Ole Opry. I find that particularly interesting since he had only been a star for a year or so. Some artists wait years before they are invited and some are never invited. Garth was humbled and honored. On the Grand Ole Opry website, he is quoted as saying "To be recognized as a member of the Grand Ole Opry is among the class of honors that will never be topped, no matter how long or how far my career goes."

Garth Brooks represented a new form of Country music. I think the Opry recognized that and wanted to jump on the bandwagon as soon as possible. There was a time when the people who played the Opry dressed in overalls and wore straw hats. The Nineties were a different time. Country had come a long way from the days of Hank Williams. Garth was leading the way. If you listen to country music today, you know that the music is much different than it was, even just in the Nineties, and it's very much different than the early years.

In 1990, Garth received more nominations for CMA Awards than anyone else. He was nominated for five awards: Male Vocalist, Single of the Year and Song of the Year (for "If Tomorrow Never Comes",) Music Video of the Year (for "The Dance"), and the Horizon Award (the artist whose career had grown the most that year.) Just after being invited to join the Opry, on October 8th, he won two of them: the Horizon Award and Music Video of the Year Award.

When he went on stage to accept the Horizon Award, he took Sandy with him. He thanked all of his heroes: George Strait, George Jones, John Wayne, and his father.

The next day, October 9, 1990, Garth was notified that *No Fences* had sold one million copies and it had only been out for five weeks.

# "UNANSWERED PRAYERS"

The next song released from *No Fences* was a song that is near and dear to my heart. "Unanswered Prayers" is probably my favorite Garth Brooks song. The song was co-written by Garth, Pat Alger, and Larry Bastian and released in October of 1990. It spent two weeks at number one on the country charts. It describes a man who attends a high school football game with his wife and runs into an old girlfriend. The girlfriend was someone he had prayed would be his girl and wife forever. Now as he looks at the girlfriend and his wife, he thanks God for unanswered prayers.

The song is based on a real incident that happened to Garth and his wife Sandy. Garth and Sandy ran into an old girlfriend one day and the incident made Garth realize how fortunate he was to have his wife. The reason this song means so much to me is the exact same thing happened to me. In 1980, I attended my 20 year high school reunion. I saw, for the first time in 20 years, the girl I had had a crush on in high school. I couldn't help but compare her to my wife and I was so grateful I had waited and that the girlfriend had rejected me. Sometimes, it's better to not get what you pray for. God knows what is best for us, even if sometimes we don't recognize it.

Next came "Two of a Kind, Workin' on a Full House" which also hit number one for one week. Garth now had three number ones in a row, but there would be more. This is a fun song which was a change after the seriousness of "Unanswered Prayers." It was written by Dennis Robbins, Bobby Boyd, and Warren Dale Haynes and was another song Garth heard years before he recorded it. I love the way he turns the word "radio" into about five syllables.

"Two of a Kind" isn't a career maker, but it is a fun song and a real crowd pleaser at his concerts. The double entendre of the words which sound straight forward, but relate to playing poker, has always intrigued me.

The fourth song from *No Fences* was "The Thunder Rolls." This would be his fifth song in succession to reach number one (sixth in total), this time for two weeks. The song was co-written by Garth and Pat Alger.

The song starts out talking about the weather, the wife sits at home worrying about her husband who is late coming home. She hopes he is OK; then he drives into the driveway. They embrace, and she smells another's perfume on him, and she knows he has cheated. Now, the thunder is not about the weather but about the feelings going on in the wife's mind.

Like "Friends in Low Places," this song has a third verse that does not appear on the album but is sung at the live concerts. The verse was deemed too intense for radio pay, so you don't hear it on the radio very often. The wife goes to her bedroom and looks into the mirror. Then she opens a drawer and takes out a pistol. She is going to make sure that she will never again wonder where he is. The insinuation is that she is going to kill him. She tells the woman in the mirror, "He won't do this again," and then the last line, "'Cause tonight will be the last time, she'll wonder where he's been."

Let me tell you, guys: don't cheat on your wife. She finds out, and you could be dead. This is classic Garth Brooks and just another of the great ones we heard at the Wynn in Las Vegas.

The video of "The Thunder Rolls" has a rocky history. Garth played the role of the cheating husband because he wanted to make sure his point was made. Sandy was upset when she found out Garth would be in the video, especially that he was doing the love scenes himself. There is also a scene of a child watching the fighting couple, and Sandy didn't like that at all. She would never watch the video. I don't know if that was the start of what would eventually be their breakup, but it's possible.

The infamous third verse is included in the video, and this caused some concern among people who thought it was condoning violence. However, it was shown to various women's groups who felt that it spoke against domestic violence and so the video was submitted to the then Nashville Network (TNN) and to Country Music Television (CMT). CMT almost immediately rated it a "pick hit" and played it for a few days. TNN played it for a short time and then decided they would only continue to play it if Garth recorded a disclaimer at the end. This Garth refused to do, so the video was pulled and never shown again. Shortly afterwards, CMT also pulled it from airplay.

Consequently, very few people actually saw the video on CMT or TNN. However, on May 7, 1991, another cable station, VH1, decided to start playing the video. I saw it there many times. Capitol Records still believed in the video and so submitted it to the Country Music Association where it was voted Video of the Year for 1991.

Garth spent the summer of 1991 touring big venues. It was during this summer that Garth developed what would become his trademark routine. The show was high in energy. Garth didn't just stand and sing. He screamed and ran around the stage. Eventually, he would hook himself to a cable and fly above the crowd. He told his friends that if the people just wanted to hear his music, they could stay home and listen to his CDs. He needed to give them a "show!" And he did. Once you see a Garth Brooks concert live, you will never forget it. It was also during this summer that he got better acquainted with Trisha Yearwood, who would play an important part in his life in the future. She was his opening act.

It was also during this summer that Garth started playing a song that wasn't country, but Garth liked very much. The song "Shameless" was written by Billy Joel and released on his *Storm Front* album in

1989. Joel did not chart with the song, but, as we'll see, Garth did wonders for the song. The intensity Garth felt when he sang the song intensified every time he sang it, screaming out "I've never been in love like this."

One more item of note happened in 1991. At the CMA Awards, Garth was voted Entertainer of the Year (for 1990), the highest award given. It was like winning the Oscar for best picture. Johnny Cash was the MC and handed him his award. This after only two albums and being in the limelight for about two years. That is truly a remarkable achievement. I don't want to get ahead of myself, but Garth won Entertainer of the Year for 1991, 1992, 1993, as well as for 1997, and 1998. Six times in a nine year period. A highlight of the evening was Garth's rendition of "Shameless" which he performed for the CMA crowd. President George H. W. Bush and wife Barbara were in the audience, and Garth practically blew the place apart with the song. Country had entered a new realm.

At the 1991 CMA Awards, Garth also won Album of the Year for *No Fences*, Single of the Year for "Friends in Low Places," and Video of the Year for "The Thunder Rolls."

# "Ropin' the Wind"

It was time for another album, his third. *Ropin' the Wind* was released on September 10, 1991 and had advanced orders of four million copies. It entered the Billboard Country Album charts and the Billboard 200 charts at number one, which was the first time that had ever happened.

It would fall out of number one, only to return again four times over the next seven months or so. Between September 28, 1991 and April 8, 1992, it spent eighteen weeks at number one on the country album charts. Garth called it "son of Fences." The album would spawn six singles, three of which would be number ones. A couple of years later, in 1993, it would be certified 14xPlatinum. In the United States, Platinum means 1 million copies sold, so that equates to 14 million records sold in two years. *Ropin' the Wind* did so well, that the sales of the first two albums increased. There was a short time when all three of Garth's albums were in the Top 20 at the same time.

There are ten songs on *Ropin' the Wind*. If you examine the list of songs on the back, there is one letter in each title that is white. The letters are SODGLSUBSE. Rearrange the letters and they spell "GOD BLESS US."

The first of those singles was "Rodeo," a song written by Larry Bastian. Bastian had written the song ten years before and its original name was "Miss Rodeo." The song was written for a female singer. He peddled it around Nashville and tried to get someone to record it but had no luck. When he had struck out for about the twentieth time, he put the song on the shelf. When Garth heard it, he, too, tried to get a women to record it. He played it for his friend Trisha Yearwood and when she rejected it, she told Garth he should record it. They had never thought of that, so they rewrote the song from a man's point of view, and it worked.

Garth likes songs where the man is in a conflict of one sort or another with the woman and "Rodeo" is one of these songs. The singer is so addicted to the rodeo life that it's like he's cheating on her with the rodeo. "Rodeo" was the first song in a year to not hit number one, peaking at number three.

After "Rodeo," Garth took a little detour and recorded a duet with his now friend Trisha Yearwood. "Like We Never Had a Broken Heart" is a beautiful song but if you look up the song on the internet, you can easily find that Garth co-wrote the song with his friend Pat Alger, but it's hard to find a reference to him actually singing on the song. Find it on YouTube and listen to it. You can hear Garth easily, and it is a beautiful duet. The song reached number four on the Country Charts. The album this song appears on, the self-titled *Trisha Yearwood* would be certified Gold within a few months of being released. This made Trisha the first woman in country music to have her debut album go gold.

The next single for Garth alone was the long awaited "Shameless," a song that he had been singing in his concerts for quite some time but had not yet recorded. It would become the seventh number one song of his career. Garth tells the story that while he was on the road, a CD of the Billy Joel album *Storm Front* was delivered to his house and when he got home, he played it. Hearing the song "Shameless," he knew right away that he wanted to record it. Garth called Billy Joel's people, and they came to an agreement, and Garth was able to record the song.

It's a much rawer, more emotional version of the song than the original, but Billy Joel liked it very much. Garth performed it at his Central Park Concert in 1997 and Billy Joel joined him on stage for "A New York Frame of Mine," another Billy Joel hit. Later in 2008, at the concert called *Last Play at Shea* (it was a concert to celebrate Shea Stadium which they were about to tear down), Garth joined Billy Joel on stage to sing "Shameless." Then again in 2011, when Garth Brooks was inducted into the *Songwriters Hall of Fame*, Billy Joel came on stage and they sang it together. The song has a rich history and, I believe, is one of Garth's best.

Garth and Sandy found out in late 1991 that they were expecting their first child.

On January 17, 1992, NBC aired *This is Garth Brooks*, the first television special to star Garth. The show did much better than expected. Well, I can't say just how much was expected, but I do know that it aired opposite a special about Michael Jackson and beat that show in the ratings. NBC was very happy. I do believe I was watching that night. It was the first time we all got a chance to see Garth in action without actually attending one of his shows.

# AWARD SEASON

During the first half of 1992, there were many award shows. First came the *American Music Awards* on January 17th. Garth won Favorite Country Male Artist, Favorite Country Single for "The Thunder Rolls," and Favorite Country Album for *No Fences.* Unfortunately, Sandy had gotten sick, and Garth was afraid for the baby. Would they lose it? No, she didn't lose it, but the doctor told her she had to stay off her feet for the next eight weeks.

In February, the *Grammy Awards* were aired from New York. Garth won Best Country Vocal Performance, Male for *Ropin' the Wind.* Sadly, because of Sandy's health, he didn't feel like he could leave her and make the trip, so he was not present to receive the award.

In March, the *People's Choice Awards* were given in Hollywood. They were hosted by Kenny Rogers, and Garth won Favorite Male Country Music Performer and Favorite Male Music Performer. The latter includes all genres of music, not just country. This shows the influence Garth was having on American music during this time. This time, Garth was able to attend and accept the awards in person.

Time marched on and in April, the *Academy of Country Music Awards* was held in Los Angeles. Sandy was much better by this time and so the two of them drove to L.A. where Garth won the Male Vocalist and (once again) Entertainer of the Year Awards. However, you might remember that this was the year when the police officers who beat Rodney King were acquitted by a jury. This action sparked riots which tore Los Angeles apart for several weeks. These riots started on the night of the *ACM Awards*, so Garth and Sandy decided to leave town right away instead of taking a chance getting caught up in the commotion.

Garth could do no wrong. Everything he touched turned to gold. On March 30, 1992, Garth made the cover of *Time* Magazine with a story about the "Country Boom." He also made the cover of *Forbes* Magazine that month with the caption "Led Zeppelin Meets Roy Rogers."

In March of 1992, Garth made his first appearance on *Saturday Night Live*.

# THE SINGLES KEEP COMING

After "Shameless," they released "What She's Doing Now" which became his next number one song. The song, also written by Garth and Pat Alger, discusses something almost everyone has thought about at one time or another. You had a boyfriend or a girlfriend and now you've broken up. You can't help but wonder what she's doing now. Is she married? Does she ever think of you? In reality, we don't know any of these things, but we do know that what she's doing now is tearing me apart.

The song was written back when Garth was pretty much unknown and Crystal Gayle actually recorded it first under the name "What's He Doing Now." She did not chart with the song, but Garth sure did.

Next was "Papa Loved Mama," written by Garth and Kim Williams, another song of cheating that is a mainstay of country music. We have a trucker who is out doing his job but leaving his wife alone back home. He would check in with her every night, but Mama needed more to hold than just a telephone, so she took to seeing other men. Papa comes home one night to surprise her and when he finds out that she's not home, he searches for her until he finds her and then kills her by driving the truck full speed into the motel room where she is having her affair.

The final words, "Mama's in the graveyard, Papa's in the Pen" tells the consequences of infidelity. Everybody loses. Garth says this was just a fun song that he had worked on before he became famous and when recording *Ropin' the Wind*, they decided to include it. "Papa Loved Mama" did not make number one, but it reached a respectable number three on the country charts.

The last single from the album was "The River," a mid-tempo song that talks about dreams and the realization of them. "The River," co-written by Garth and Victoria Shaw, was his ninth single to hit number one. Garth called it "a song of inspiration." He later said that of all the letters he receives, most of them are about "The River."

On July 8, 1992, Garth's world was turned upside down with the birth of his and Sandy's first daughter. They named her Taylor Mayne Pearl Brooks. The name Taylor is after Garth's favorite singer as he was growing up, James Taylor. Mayne is a convoluted spelling of the state Maine, which was where little Taylor was conceived. Sandy was a big fan of the country icon Minnie Pearl and so the third name was Pearl. Like anyone who has a baby for the first time, Garth's life would never be the same.

Some say that Garth was not the same after his daughter's birth. His live shows were toned down and not as wild as they had been. He didn't perform the antics that he was so well known for. Being a father had a profound effect on Garth. It was during this period of his life that he came very close to quitting the business altogether. He knew he didn't need the money anymore. He had done so well in the last two years that he could retire and just take care of his family. Fortunately for us and the music that came from Garth after 1993, he did not do that.

He got involved in charitable projects. He started collecting food at his concerts, providing the food for the *Feed the Children* charity. Helping others was a given for Garth. There were times when he got so many requests for personal help that he just couldn't keep up. He was actually criticized by some when he didn't get a chance to help someone who was in trouble. There just wasn't enough hours in the day.

# "THE CHASE"

Garth's next album was *The Chase* which was only his fourth album, so far, released on September 22, 1992. Not many performers can say they are a super star with just four albums. The album debuted at number one on both the Billboard country charts and on the Billboard Hot 200.

The first single that was released from *The Chase* was "We Shall Be Free" which was actually released before the album came out. It was written as a direct result of Garth's feelings after he happened to be in Los Angeles during the Watts riots of 1992. The song talks about freedom for everyone, people of all color and all ages and all sexual orientations. That last part is a familiar anthem today but not so much in 1992. A lot has happened in 20 years, but in 1992, tolerance for the Gay and Lesbian community was not even as strong as it is today, and we know they are still fighting today.

This is easily the most controversial song Garth ever recorded, and it suffered a little because of that. The song only reached number twelve on the charts, a poor showing after all of his number ones. The video for the song did win Video of the Year at the *1993 ACM Awards*.

Toward the end of 1992, Garth released his first Christmas album called *Beyond the Season*. The album did very well, peaking at number two on the Country Album Charts and on the Billboard Hot 200 chart. Most of the songs on the album are traditional Christmas music like "White Christmas" and "Silent Night." One song that stands out is "The Old Man's Back in Town" which was co-written by Garth and was released as a single with "Santa Looks a Lot Like Daddy" on the reverse side. "Daddy" is an old song that Buck Owens recorded back in 1965. They are both fun songs that if you listen to country radio, you'll still hear them played to this day around the holidays.

In December of 1992, they announced that *Ropin' the Wind* was the number one album of the entire year. That did not just include country but all genres. He was the number one period. The American people were embracing Garth Brooks like no other country artist before him. The cherry on top was that *No Fences* was number six. Thus, Garth had two of the top ten albums of the year. Garth was the top performer in the United States and country had taken over pop as the prominent genre of music. 1993 was looking to be a very good year.

He was back on top with "Somewhere Other Than the Night" which was his next single, co-written by Garth and his buddy Kent Blazy. It debuted on the charts on October 17, 1992 and hit number one on January 13, 1993 for one week. This song is a ballad, and Garth is as good at ballads as he is at the up tempo tunes. The song is basically a love song and includes the line about when the man comes home and finds his wife with nothing but her apron on. That is what every man (OK, maybe not) wants to see when he comes home from work.

Next came "Learning to Live Again," which peaked at number two. This song didn't mean much to me in 1993 but a few years later after my marriage had ended and I was single again and trying to re-enter the dating world after 28 years of marriage, this song spoke directly to me. A man who has lost a first love, either through death or divorce, we're not told, is trying to re-enter the dating world. He goes out on a double-date with some friends. He tries to dance and he can't remember her name. The night goes well until they are on her front porch saying goodnight. He kisses her on the cheek and asks if he can see her again. It's then that she reveals that she is learning to live again as well and she coyly responds, "We'll see." Yes, learning to live again can be rough.

"That Summer" is an old story of a young boy with an older experienced woman. Rod Stewart told the same story in his hit "Maggie May" back in 1971. As the song progresses, the boy grows up and remembers his first time. A boy never forgets his first time, no matter who she was. The song brought Garth back to the top of the charts.

In 1993, Garth was asked to be a part of the Barbara Walters interview show. She had a weekly program in which she interviewed different celebrities and had been after Garth for a year or so to be on the show. He finally agreed. During the interview, Walters asked him about the song "We Shall Be Free" and the controversy that surrounded it. Barbara was always after a good story. She was particularly interested in the line about people being able to love anyone they please. Garth announced on the show that his sister Betsy was gay and that he still loved her and thought she had a right to love just like anyone else.

Well, you can imagine the uproar that resulted because of Garth outing his sister on national television, but Betsy was good with it. People's minds were changing, and there wasn't any backlash from the comment.

# "IN PIECES"

In August of 1993, *In Pieces* was released. Garth says the album was called that because it kind of came together from a lot of places and had to be pieced together. Like its predecessor, it also debuted at number one on both album charts. Also, it became Garth's biggest album in Great Britain as the fans across the pond where finally catching up with America in their love of Garth Brooks.

The album is what they call in the industry, "a shit-kicker." The songs are louder and more energetic. Garth says this album is closer to a live album than anything they had done up to this point. The band was playing well together. They had been together now for about four years and they knew each other and what was needed to produce a great song. The first single from the album was "Ain't Goin' Down ('Til the Sun Comes Up)," a rocking' number that is more rock and roll than it is country. It was released in July of 1993. The story is a familiar one: the teenager going out for a night on the town with her boyfriend. Mama says she better be back by dawn (I bet your Mother never let you stay out that late.) Of course, they don't make it. They don't get back until after the sun comes up. Mama grounds the girl, but that doesn't make any difference, the next night she's off again. Typical teenage rebellion that was as prevalent in the Nineties as it was in any other era. It's a really fun song to listen to and got the crowd moving when he did it live.

The song spent two weeks at number one (not consecutive) and was a great kickoff for the new album. It was also number one in Canada and got up to thirteen in Great Britain.

Next they released "American Honky-Tonk Bar Association" which has been compared to "Friends in Low Places." It has the same appeal and is another rocker and came out in September of 1993. It was written by Bryan Kennedy and Jim Rushing, both of whom were good friends of Garth. The song was originally called "American Redneck Bar Association," but the name was changed when Garth recorded it.

The song is basically a celebration of the common man, the man who farms, the construction worker, or the truck driver. All of these are members of the "American Honky-Tonk Bar Association" or as Garth calls it, the AHBA. Garth was telling these people that they could do something about their situation, that everyone could make things better if they tried. Just go join the AHBA. Garth got some criticism about the line that refers to welfare recipients, but nothing he couldn't handle. This was yet another number one song, but it was his last number one for almost two years.

1993 would continue to be a standout year for Garth as he next released "Standing Outside the Fire." This song would break his string of number ones and "only" reached number three. He wrote the song with a Los Angeles friend, Jenny Yates. The song is meant to be inspirational. It talks about taking risks and making life worthwhile by jumping in and accomplishing things. The video for this song is easily one of the best Garth has ever done. It shows an autistic high school boy who is determined to race against the regular kids in a track meet. It seems his mother is the only one who believes in him. During the race he falls and his Dad comes on the field and encourages him to get up and continue running even though he is hurt. The boy gets up and finishes the race. It brought tears to my eyes. We can do anything if we set our minds to it. The video was available on YouTube as of this writing. I hope it's still there so you can watch it. You won't be sorry.

Maybe the public was so used to the up tempo, rocking kind of songs that when "One Night a Day" came out, it wasn't received as well as the former songs. The song is a ballad and, I think, a beautiful song. It includes only four instruments, the piano (which Garth plays), saxophone (played by Jim Horn), a bass guitar, and drums. The song, which would have been a huge success by anyone else, was kind of a letdown for Garth, peaking at only number seven.

His next song didn't even make the Top 40, but I have to mention it because it is a perfect example of the melting of country and rock. "Hard Luck Woman" was a song originally recorded by the rock group Kiss back in 1976. Written by Paul Stanley originally for Rod Stewart, he decided to keep it for Kiss. In 1994, Garth had the opportunity to record the song with Kiss for their tribute album *Kiss My Ass: Classic Kiss Regrooved.* Garth was joined by Kiss on the record which did not do well as a single, only peaking at number 67, but it was still one of those moments in rock and country music that you never forget.

His next hit was "Callin' Baton Rouge" which returns us to the more up tempo rocking (sort of) theme that people were used to by this time. "Callin' Baton Rouge" has quite a history. It was recorded by the Oak Ridge Boys back in 1978. It was then covered by the band New Grass Revival, who had several chart hits in the late Eighties, but "Callin' Baton Rouge" was their only top 40 song which reached number 37 in 1989.

Garth decided to cover the song for *In Pieces,* and he asked New Grass Revival to join him on the record. New Grass had broken up about a year earlier and this was an opportunity to get back together and play again. Garth says he had always been a fan of the band. Each successive version of this song gets more rowdy until we get to Garth's which is the rowdiest of all. It reached number two on the singles charts.

I could leave *In Pieces* now, but I'd like to mention one more song. "The Red Strokes" was the last single released from the album and while it was not a hit (peaking at number 49), it is memorable to me because of the video. You can listen to the song and enjoy it, it's a beautiful song. But the video is so powerful. Garth is dressed in a white tuxedo with a white cowboy hat, playing a white piano in a white room. As he plays and sings, red paint splashes over the white surfaces. It's a stunning effect. It is my understanding that real paint was used in making the video (probably, the water soluble kind.) Garth is literally immersed in it. It required 18 tuxedos, 12 hats, and eight pianos to get the video filmed. The red goo consisted of 5000 gallons of mud mixed with 35 gallons of red paint. What a mess.

But it was worth it. Garth won Best Video of the Year at the *1995 ACM Awards*. Things were beginning to slow down for Garth. That was the only award he won that year. To show Garth's increasing fan base in Great Britain, "The Red Strokes" was the first song of his to reach the Top 40 Pop charts in England. Not country, but pop. That was a remarkable feat.

# TEXAS STADIUM

The home of the Dallas Cowboys, Texas Stadium has been the site for some moments in American History that we will never forget. Remember the Coca-Cola ad that played during the Superbowl and showed a young boy offering his Coke to Mean Joe Greene, a former All-Pro defensive tackle for the Pittsburg Steelers? The ramp that is shown in the ad now resides in Texas Stadium in Arlington, Texas.

There are many more things I could say about Texas Stadium, but I'm here to talk about Garth Brooks and he performed probably the single greatest Country concert ever given at Texas Stadium or anywhere else for that matter.

Garth literally took over the stadium for about two weeks to set up his show. It was the most elaborate setup Texas had ever seen. Stage hands were hurt putting it together. Nobody seriously, but enough so that Garth was really concerned that he was putting lives in danger by doing this show. It went forward, however, and on Friday, September 24, 1993, the first of three sold-out concerts was held at Texas Stadium to the delight of several thousands of people.

Garth came out on stage in front of 65,000 roaring fans and announced that they were there to, "Raise some hell." The crowd screamed their approval. NBC filmed the show, and it became Garth's second television special, *"This is Garth Brooks II"* which aired later in May of 1994.

What followed can only be described as an extravaganza. He sang "Standing Outside the Fire" and there were flames on the stage. A minor mishap actually set Garth on fire but luckily it was caught and no damage was done. Lightening lit up the sky during different numbers and then the moment that no one there would ever forget. Garth's hit that was on the charts at the time was "Ain't Goin' Down

('Til the Sun Comes Up)" and when he started singing that song, suddenly, he was flying.

Garth, suspended by two wires, soured over the crowd and gave everyone a close-up view of him, even those who were in the nose bleed seats way in the back. It was a spectacle that no one had seen before. I'm pretty sure this is the first time Garth had ever done this stunt, and it would become a regular part of his concerts from then on. What was remarkable about this is not the technology, which certainly existed in 1993, the important thing was that Garth Brooks is afraid of heights. He was willing to suspend that fear to put on a show for his fans. I had heard of this, of course, and that was one reason I expected to see something like that when I went to Las Vegas to see him in person. But, of course, that didn't happen.

This concert at Texas Stadium on a hot September evening in 1993 still, to this day, holds the record for attendance of a country music event by a single artist.

# FIRST INTERNATIONAL TOUR

By 1994, Garth was a household word in the United States, and it seemed like he had been around forever. However, as much as he had toured the U.S., he had never been overseas. Talking with his people, it was decided that Ireland would be a good place to start a European tour. Thus, off went Garth and the band to Dublin. He was pleasantly surprised that the people there knew his music and could sing along with almost every song. After conquering Ireland, he next went to Birmingham, England and London's Wembley Arena to play to sold-out crowds. The British media didn't know what to make of Garth. They expected a cowboy to walk through the door packing a six-shooter and Garth just didn't fit the profile. One London disc-jockey called him Garth Vader.

Then it was on to Switzerland, the Netherlands, and other countries before returning back home. The tour was a smashing success. He decided that he would do it again, so he spent the summer of 1994 rehearsing and preparing for a second tour which included New Zealand, Australia, and then back to Europe to visit Spain, Germany, and France and then to visit England one more time.

I can't forget one other really important thing that happened in 1994. Garth and Sandy had their second daughter. August Anna was born on May 4, 1994. Luckily, Garth was between his two world tours so he could be home for the birth.

Things were already beginning to slow down for Garth. He wanted to stay home and take care of his two girls. He wanted to see then grow up. The seeds of retirement had already been planted, even though they would not germinate for a few more years. When you look at a list of Garth's hits, there is a gap from August, 1994 until September, 1995 when there are no hits. Garth just wasn't recording. Being, basically a simple man with simple needs, I suspect Garth felt like he had made as much money as he needed and could relax. During the *22nd annual American Music Awards*, held on January 30, 1995, Garth won for Best Country Male Artist, even though he had not released an album of new material in 1994. He told the crowd, he missed them and was taking 1995 off from performing but, he said, "I may not be able to wait. I miss you all."

His record company did release his first collection of Greatest Hits in 1994, called *The Garth Brooks Collection* which had ten songs that were listed as "favorites" of Garth. It was available only at McDonald's restaurants and $1 of every sale went to the Ronald McDonald House fund. This was a way Garth could give back to the communities.

Another album of hits was released in December of 1994. This one was on sale at normal music stores, and it contained everything that he had recorded up to this point. Called just *The Hits*, Garth really didn't like greatest hits albums and asked that it be pulled from the stores. By the time they got around to doing that, it had debuted at number one on both Billboard charts and went on to sell ten million copies. You can find the album on Amazon, but it's only sold by third party vendors who are asking over $50 for a new copy. It's now officially listed as "Out of Print."

In February of 1993, *No Fences* reported sales of 13 Million, making it the highest selling album in the history of country music.

In the summer of 1995, Ty England, who had been with Garth's band almost from the beginning, released his first solo album, the self-titled *Ty England*. The hit song "Should've asked Her Faster" was a big hit for Ty, hitting number three on the country charts. Unfortunately, he was never able to do it again.

# "FRESH HORSES"

Garth spent much of 1995 working on the songs for his next album, called *Fresh Horses*. It was released in November of 1995 and did make number one on the Billboard Country Album charts but just peaked at number two on the Hot 200 chart.

Something that I have never seen before is that almost every song on the *Fresh Horses* album debuted on the Billboard charts simultaneously. I think the record company releases the songs for radio play, but they are not available as singles yet. Since the country charts track air-play, they appear on the charts as hits. Almost every song is shown as debuting on December 9, 1995. Not all of them were hits, but some were. The first to strike gold was "She's Every Woman" which went to number one. This song and the one that followed ("The Fever") are exceptions to the same day rule, since they were released before the album to gather advance sales.

"She's Every Woman" is a tribute to all women. I can't help but think he might be singing about Sandy. Any man who is in love with a woman will understand the words to this song. In 1995, I think Garth and Sandy were still a happy couple. Garth co-wrote the song with Victoria Shaw, the woman who co-wrote the classic "The River."

As I said, next came "The Fever" which is an Aerosmith song that they recorded just a couple years earlier for their *Get a Grip* album. Garth does a great imitation of Steven Tyler singing this song. You can hear Tyler in the sound of the song. Garth changed some of the words so that it's about a rodeo rider who has to keep a firm grip on the rope when he's riding the bull. It sounds like Aerosmith is singing more about being high on drugs which is something Garth wouldn't sing about. The public didn't quite go along for the ride, however, since the song only peaked at number 23.

"The Beaches of Cheyenne" was the next release from *Fresh Horses* and, believe it or not, it started out to be a light hearted, almost funny song, but it sure didn't end up that way. The song describes a cowboy who is killed while riding the bulls in a rodeo. His wife is so grief stricken that she walks into the ocean and drowns. It then talks about the ghost of the woman who walks "The Beaches of Cheyenne." Quite a sad song.

"The Beaches of Cheyenne" did hit number one for one week, but it would be the last number one for Garth for almost two years. There were three more singles released from *Fresh Horses*, but none of them hit number one. "It's Midnight Cinderella" was the next song to reach the Top 40 where it peaked at number five. It was one of six songs from the album (including "The Beaches of Cheyenne") that were all released as album cuts back in December of 1995. "It's Midnight Cinderella" did not peak until September of 1996.

It was followed by "The Change" which paid tribute to the victims of the Oklahoma City bombing in 1995. It barely made the top 20, peaking at number 19. Then there was "The Old Stuff" (#64) and "Rollin'" (#71) and finally "That Ol' Wind" (#75).

"That Ol' Wind" was re-released to radio stations in September of 1996, and this time it peaked at number four. This was more than a year after it had charted the first time. This is a familiar story. A young woman with a child hears about a rock star that is coming to town for one last concert. She reunites with the performer, not telling him that he is the father of her child. It's a nice song, which Garth handles in true Garth fashion.

1995 was not a terribly busy year for Garth. Songs were released, and his name was kept in front of the public, but he didn't tour, and he didn't record any new music. In January of 1996 when the *American Music Awards* came around again, Garth won the top prize of the night: Artist of the Year. He had previously won the Favorite Country

Male Artist Award and had accepted that but when he won the Artist of the Year, he felt that he didn't deserve it. He told the crowd: "With no disrespect to the show and to Dick Clark, I'm going to leave the award right here." And he left it on the podium and walked away.

Why didn't he think he deserved it? I guess he felt that he really hadn't done much in 1995. There were artists much more deserving of the award. The *AMAs* decided a short time later that the award would become a "travelling" award. They put Garth's name on it, but it would be there for just one year and then passed on to the next recipient.

In May of 1996, Garth moved into first place among solo acts for sales of records. He passed the 60 million sales mark. The previous leader had been Billy Joel with 57 million sales, but Garth was number one. The only act ahead of him was the Beatles who had sold 71 million albums. Of course, the Beatles were not recording any more as a group, so their record was in jeopardy. This data comes from the RIAA, who keeps track of things like that, but they had completely overlooked Elvis Presley, who was far ahead of either the Beatles or Garth Brooks.

Then, a couple months later, on July 28, 1996, little Allie Colleen Brooks was born. This was Garth's third daughter and her middle name is obviously named after Garth's mother.

In early 1997, Garth went on tour again back to Ireland and other parts of Europe. The people knew him better this time. He was well received and sold out where ever he went. As usual, he took his family with him everywhere he went. This time, his mother Colleen came along. She had Irish heritage and was especially thrilled to be on Irish soil where her ancestors had grown up.

# "SEVENS"

Garth's seventh album was, appropriately, called *Sevens*. They really took advantage of the seven number. Milking the number for all they could, they designated 777,777 copies of the CD as "First Edition" with a special seal on the case. I would have thought that the designation would have increased the value of the album but not so much. You can buy the first edition version of the CD on Amazon now for about $17 which isn't that far from what it sold for originally.

*Sevens* was supposed to come out in August of 1997, but there was a shakeup in management at Capital Records, and the album got delayed until November. Garth was set to play a concert in Central Park, New York City that same month and had hoped to promote the new album at that concert and when the album didn't get released on time, he was very unhappy. His career was slowing down, and he wasn't adjusting to it very well. *Fresh Horses* had not sold as well as his previous albums, and he was worried that the public might be getting tired of him.

But, as they say in show business, "The show must go on," and Garth Brooks was a professional and so moved forward despite the setbacks.

The concert in Central Park went on as planned. A lot of people wondered if New Yorkers would come out for a country concert. After all, some big talent had played Central park, including Barbra Streisand, Simon & Garfunkel, and Diana Ross. Could Garth compete with that? They had nothing to worry about. On August 7, 1997, people started coming into the park early in the morning and stayed the entire day until the concert started. During the day, Mayor Rudolph Giuliani presented Garth with a crystal Apple (the Big Apple) and proclaimed August 7th as Garth Brooks' Day in New York City.

Garth was nervous, but he had done this so many times before that he soon got into the groove and had the crowd eating out of his hand. During the concert, Billy Joel joined him on stage to sing a couple of songs and then at the end of the night, as if it couldn't get any better, Don MacLean joined him to sing "American Pie," a song with which Garth would often sing to end his concerts. This was a night Garth would never forget.

A song that filled in the time gap on the charts was "In Another's Eyes," a duet he recorded with his friend Trisha Yearwood. The song was co-written by Garth, Bobby Wood, and John Peppard. At the time this came out, I felt this was a Trisha Yearwood song and Garth was just helping out. But that's not really true. Listen to the song and you'll see that they each have about equal time on the song. It was included on *Sevens* as well as Yearwood's seventh album (there's the number seven again) called *(Songbook) A Collection of Hits* which, as the name implies, was a greatest hits collection for her.

*Sevens* was officially released on November 25, 1997 and even though it had been two years since he had put out an album, it took off like a rocket. Garth was worried that the public had forgotten him during the time he was inactive. I remember that time, and I know it didn't even occur to me that it had been two years since we had seen a new album from Garth. It just felt like, hey, great, he's back and has new stuff. Let's go buy it. *Sevens* ended up selling 28xDiamond worldwide.

I think one of the reasons the album did so well is that it felt like Garth was back to his roots again. After the duet with Trisha Yearwood, which really felt more like her song than his, he put out two drinking songs that were pure country. One of the basic themes of country music is drinking and getting drunk. The first of these was "Long Necked Bottle," a familiar story of a man sitting in the bar drinking a "long necked bottle" while his gal is at home waiting for him. It's a fun song and, I feel, a little more traditional than other songs he had been recording. It was co-written by Steve Wariner who was a country star himself (although not of the scale of Garth.) I can't find any evidence that Wariner recorded this himself, although there is a video on YouTube of him and Garth singing the song. It spent three weeks at number one in late 1996. I think the people were glad to have Garth back.

Another drinking song followed. "Two Piña Coladas" is the story of a depressed man who goes down to the sea to forget his troubles. He orders two piña coladas (one for each hand) and pretty soon he is feeling no pain. The song goes on to explain that with the help of Captain Morgan (a brand of rum), all of his troubles will go away. This song also reached number one both in the United States and Canada.

"She's Gonna Make It" is a song about a couple who are breaking up and how hard it is on the two of them. Garth sings that she's gonna make it but he never will. The song might be considered a prophesy of what was to come in Garth's life in just a couple of years.

These were the only four songs from *Sevens* to enter the Top 40. The rest of the album was released to radio stations for airplay, but nothing else clicked with the public.

Sometimes, it doesn't matter how many hits you have from a certain album, the public loves you anyway. Garth Brooks was loved by the public and no matter how many hits or misses he had, that would never change. In 1997, he was awarded Entertainer of the Year for the fifth time at the *American Country Music Awards*. This was his first award since 1993, so it meant a lot to him; however, he wasn't in town but was, as usual, out on tour, so someone else had to accept the award for him.

He won Entertainer of the Year again in 1998, making it two years in a row and six times total.

# THE LIMITED SERIES

With all his success, Garth had never released a box-set of his music, so in May of 1998, his record label Capital Nashville released *The Limited Series*, which included the first six albums Garth recorded. (It did not include *Sevens*.) Now, you may know that record companies will sometimes release a Greatest Hits album and then include a new single that has never been heard before just to get the real fans to buy the music again so while *The Limited Series* included all six albums, each album had an extra song that no one had heard before; thus, making the set an instant collector's item.

*The Limited Series* debuted at number one on both the Billboard Hot 200 and the Country Albums charts. This is the first box-set to ever debut on two charts. It also set a record for sales in the first week of 372,410 copies. Sales were limited to two million copies in the United States (thus, the name *The Limited Series*.)

The extra song included on the *Fresh Horses* CD was "To Make You Feel My Love." This song deserves special mention because it was another number one single for Garth, and it was written by Bob Dylan for his 1998 album *Time Out of Mind*. The song is also featured on the soundtrack of the movie *Hope Floats* which starred Sandra Bullock. This is a beautiful song which is perfect for Garth Brooks. It was Garth's first song to cross over to the Adult Contemporary Chart. The song was also covered by Billy Joel. Bob Dylan himself later released it as a single, but it did not chart.

It was about this time that Garth Brooks came to Salt Lake City where I was living. Unfortunately, I had a job that took me away from home from Monday until Friday, so when I got home on Friday, I had to catch up with the news of the week. One week, I came home to find out that Garth was coming to town and that tickets were going on sale that very Friday morning. Well, I didn't get home until evening on Friday and so when I tried to get tickets, they were sold out. I heard later that they had sold out in less than 30 minutes. He even added another show and that also sold out quickly. All of this while I was blissfully unaware in another city. I was so mad. I had missed my opportunity to see Garth Brooks live. He never came to Salt Lake City again.

On November 17, 1998, Garth tried something that had never been done before. He wanted to sell a million copies of an album in its first week. The album was *Double Live,* and it had pre-sale orders of 6.8 million copies. If he could get the public to buy at least one million in the first week it was released, he would break the record set by the Soundtrack to the movie *The Bodyguard* in 1993. Garth went on *The Tonight Show* to promote the album. He arranged a live feed of the album to Walmart stores and during the first week of release, he sold 1,085,000 copies to set the record for more than one million albums sold. Quite an accomplishment.

# CHRIS GAINES

In 1999, Garth was proclaimed The Artist of the Decade by the *Academy of Country Music*. This award has only been given four times (as of 1999) with Marty Robbins receiving it for the Sixties, Loretta Lynn for the Seventies, and Alabama for the Eighties. All candidates for a Legends of Country Music book. It's beyond the scope of this book, but just for your information, George Strait was awarded the award for the first decade of the 2000s. We are only about half way through the second decade of the 2000s, but my money is on Miranda Lambert or Blake Sheldon for this decade's award (maybe Luke Bryant.)

At any rate, Garth won it for the Nineties.

Then Garth proceeded to enter into one of the strangest agreements of his, or anyone else's, career. He decided to record an album as an alter-ego named Chris Gaines. He intended to record an album called *Garth Brooks ...In the Life of Chris Gaines*, so there was no hiding the fact that he was Gaines, but why did he do it? This definitely comes under the category of "What was he thinking?"

He hooked up with Paramount Pictures who was planning a movie called *The Lamb* which would feature Chris Gaines (Garth playing the part.) The album has purported to be a sort of Greatest Hits album containing songs from the five previous albums Chris Gaines had released. The only problem was, Gaines had never released any albums, let alone five. He was a product of Garth's imagination. All this did was confuse the public. Garth had always wanted to be in films, and he thought *The Lamb* was the vehicle to get him there. He had seen other country stars appear in films: Trace Adkins had done it and so had Tim McGraw.

A single was released from the album called "Lost in You" which is a pretty good song. You can find it on YouTube. It wasn't even given to country stations; Garth wanted to make it in the pop world. Well, even though the song is good, it didn't make it. It did make the country charts, at number 62, but that was it. It was a bold and inventive experiment, but it just didn't work. Garth said he knew it was a risk. He said the public would either get it or they won't. They didn't.

I think people were too used to Garth being who he was and this departure into the weird was just not in keeping with the image they had of him. Chris Gaines died a quick death and nothing more was ever mentioned of him. The movie that was to be made, *The Lamb*, came into some financial and managerial problems and that, too, was scraped.

To add to Garth's problems, the mother who he loved almost more than anyone else in the world, passed away after a long fight with throat cancer. She died on August 6, 1999. She was seventy.

# IT'S OVER. OR IS IT?

On December 15, 1999, Garth appeared on the *Crook & Chase* show which aired on The Nashville Network (TNN) and announced that he would be retiring at the end of 2000. Actually what he said was that he would announce his retirement in the next year, so this was an announcement for an announcement. He said music was just not his highest priority any more. He had three daughters, Allie, three, August, five, and Taylor, seven. He had been away from home too much, and he wanted to see his daughters grow up. Also, there were rumors that all was not well in the Brooks home. He and Sandy were having "unspecified" problems.

The death of his mother made him realize just how important a parent is in a child's life. His girls needed him, and he needed to be with them. Taylor was learning soccer and needed a Dad to step in and teach her how it was done.

The failure of Chris Gaines and the death of his mother made 1999 about as bad a year as 1998 had been good. Garth was down for the count and wondering what happened. The news of Garth's retirement was all they were talking about in Nashville and elsewhere. What would Garth do with himself, just stay home and take care of the family? Garth said that he intended to stay busy. He still wanted to make a film and had some ideas for that. Even though *The Lamb* hadn't worked out, there were other possibilities.

One big question that the record companies talked about was who would replace Garth? He was selling 10% of the records coming out of Nashville, and they would take a big hit when he quit. It turned out that no one could completely fill Garth's shoes, but there was a whole new generation of country singers coming up that were very capable of, at least partially, filling them. People like Keith Urban, Brad Paisley, Tim McGraw, Faith Hill, and Shania Twain.

At home, Garth's marriage was in trouble. Things were not good between him and Sandy and Garth thought that by retiring and getting off the road, he could fix that. But it was not to be. They had separated in March of 1999 but didn't announce their plans to divorce until October 9, 2000. I think they worked on it during that time, but the division was just too great. They finally filed for divorce on November 6, 2000, and it became final on December 17. They remained friends, and the divorce was not a bitter one. Garth says they needed to remain parents, they didn't want to remain married. They even moved into separate farms which were just down the road from one another.

Late 2000 was bitter-sweet for Garth as in October, Capital Records held a party to celebrate his reaching 100 million albums sold in his career. Now, I've read in various places that this was a record for a solo artist, but I think they must mean a record in the country music genre. I know that Elvis Presley is far and away the King of selling records as it is estimated that he has sold over 2.5 Billion records during and after his life, and that is a number no one will probably ever reach again. The Beatles are in second place (although not a solo act) with 1.6 Billion records worldwide. But Garth had only been active for about ten years and both Elvis and the Beatles had been around for decades.

# "SCARECROW"

Garth owed Capital one more record before he could retire. He got together with his people and tried to find songs that he could include on the album; it took some time. There was a three year gap between studio album number seven *Sevens* and studio album number eight. (Not counting Chris Gaines.) *Scarecrow* was released on November 13, 2001. This was just two months after 9-11 and like several of those before it, it debuted at number one on both charts. This was the seventh time that had happened. Even though the album was a success, I think the people were beginning to look elsewhere for country music. In 1999, the Entertainer of the Year was Shania Twain who was really hot (in more ways than one) at this time. The Dixie Chicks took the award in 2000 and Garth did not appear at all in the list of awards. I'm not sure if the detour into Chris Gaines had been good for his career.

*Scarecrow* would be the last studio album Garth would do. So far, this is 2014, and there has not been another one. Garth says they named the album after the scarecrow in *The Wizard of Oz*; he was all heart and no brains and Garth says that is the way he felt.

The first single from *Scarecrow* has an interesting history. Remember the movie *Frequency*? It stars Jim Caviezel as a man who is suddenly able to talk to his dead father, Dennis Quaid, 30 years in the past. It is easily one of my favorite movies of all time. The movie was supposed to have a soundtrack, and they asked Garth Brooks to write a song for it. Having lost his mother just a year earlier, he wrote "When You Come Back to Me Again" which is dedicated to his mother. The soundtrack idea was dropped, but the song did appear in the movie and it resulted in a Golden Globe for Best Original Song.

Garth decided to make a video of the song as a tribute to his mother. When the video was released, radio stations liked it so much that they stripped the audio from the video and played the song. Well, if it was going to be played anyway, it might as well be on the album, so it was the first release from *Scarecrow*. It reached number 21 on the country charts. While this is not Garth's biggest hit, it's one of his most powerful and one of my personal favorites. I still get chills today listening to "When You Come Back to Me Again."

The second single from *Scarecrow* was the fun song "Beer Run (B-double-E-double-Are-You-In)" a duet he did with George Jones. What's more country than singing about beer? It's about two friends who live in a dry county and have to drive across the county line to buy beer. It will get your foot tapping. The song was not a huge hit by Garth Brook's standards, but it got up to number 24 on the Country Top 40.

The biggest hit from *Scarecrow* was "Wrapped Up In You" which was the second release from the album. It's an up tempo love song that is pretty generic. It's a pleasant tune and peaked at number five on the charts.

Next was another duet, this time with his old partner, Trisha Yearwood. "Squeeze Me In" did manage to squeeze into position sixteen on the country charts, but that's as high as it got.

I know there are people that find it hard to believe that Trisha Yearwood wasn't the real reason Garth and Sandy got divorced, but it really wasn't. They had been friends for years, but it was never taken to the next step. In 1999, Yearwood also got divorced from her husband Robert Reynolds. She needed a shoulder to cry on and Garth was there. During the taping of "Squeeze Me In," they got closer than they had ever been.

The relationship just matured from there. Garth realized that this was what he wanted for the rest of his life. They kept things secret until early 2002, when the relationship became public and they started seeing each other openly.

# RETIREMENT

As an outsider, it seemed to me that when Garth retired, he really did "leave the building." I know I didn't hear much about him after about 2001. But, Garth was busy. He was busy being a father to his girls. He says he made them breakfast every morning and gradually learned to be a pretty good cook. He and Sandy lived on near-by farms and saw each other frequently. Each of them were able to see their children every day.

His relationship with Trisha Yearwood blossomed, and they became closer and closer until he realized he was in love with her. I heard him say on television that he considered Trisha his "soul mate." This often happens in second marriages. It happened to me. I am much closer to my second wife than I ever was with my first, but that's just the way it works sometimes.

When he felt it was right, Garth formally proposed to Trisha. He did it like a man should, down on one knee and in public. They were at the unveiling of The Legends in Bronze, a sculpture of eight country singers (one of them was Garth) at Buck Owen's Crystal Palace in Bakersfield, California. Trisha, flustered, said yes and everyone cheered.

They were married on December 10, 2005. They are still together as of this writing.

In 2004, tragedy hit again when Garth found out that his life-long idol, Chris LeDoux, was very sick. Garth had been friends with LeDoux for most of his career and he was devastated to hear that LeDoux was diagnosed with bile duct cancer. He needed a liver transplant, and Garth was first in line to offer a piece of his, but, unfortunately, he was not a match. Eventually, nothing could be done for Chris LeDoux and in March of 2005, he died.

I remember very well when this happened. I was a big Chris LeDoux fan also and the first thing I did was go buy all of his albums I could get. Garth and Chris had been close ever since Garth's very first song "Much Too Young" which talks about a worn out tape of Chris LeDoux being the only friend he had on the road. Garth wanted badly to come out of retirement to record a tribute to LeDoux but didn't see how to do that without touring, and he wasn't ready for that yet. Luckily, fate stepped in and found a way.

Walmart had approached Garth with the proposition that they put together an album called *The Lost Sessions* (the album was later included in a larger set called *The Limited Series*, the same name as the first box set Garth released in 1998.) The set would sell only at the Walmart stores. This set would consist of recordings that he had made over the years that hadn't yet made it to the public. They were, basically, lost music. He wouldn't have to do promotions for it; Walmart would do that, he wouldn't have to tour, and, best of all, he could add a new song to the collection. My wife gave me this set for Christmas in 2005. It was one of my favorite presents, and I still listen to it to this day.

His contract with Capital had just run out, so he was a free man and he controlled his own music. He could do what he wanted with it. It was the perfect answer. He included a new song "Good Ride Cowboy," written by Jerrod Neimann, Bryan Kennedy, Richie Brown, and Bob Doyle. This is a fun up tempo song that is Garth's tribute to Chris LeDoux. For us, as fans, it was the first new Garth Brooks in five years. It peaked at number three on the country charts.

The next year, 2006, Walmart was back. They had done so well the first time, why don't we try it again? They released another set called *The Ultimate Hits*. This was not technically a box set, just a double CD, the third such compilation Garth had released. This set had two noteworthy songs, both of which I like very much.

They released "More Than a Memory" which debuted as a single at number one on the Billboard Country Charts. It was the first and still is, the only song to have ever done that. Garth has had lots of number ones and so have many other people, but not until that day in 2005 had anyone debuted at number one. "More Than a Memory" is a nice song, but I don't think it is Garth's best. However, people were so hungry for Garth Brooks material that this song started out on top.

The song is a love lost song, written from the viewpoint of a man who has lost his love and has tried to forget but just can't because she's, "More Than a Memory."

They next released a song which just tickled me. I am a huge Huey Lewis fan. I enjoy rock and roll as much as country and have written about many rock performers. I haven't gotten to Huey Lewis yet, but I will, someday. "Workin' For a Living" was first introduced on Huey Lewis and the News' album *Picture This*. It was a single for them and just barely missed hitting the Top 40, peaking at number 41. I do remember the video, however, as MTV was hot then and everybody was making videos.

I'm not sure what brought Huey Lewis and Garth together, but I'm glad it did. They did "Workin' for a Living" for *The Ultimate Hits* album and recorded a video for the duet which shows them standing in the middle of a NASCAR race with cars speeding by them at high rates of speed. I can't tell if they are really there or if it's just computer magic, but if they are there, they are taking their lives in their hands to shoot a video, but they seem to be having fun doing it. The song reached number 15 on the Billboard Country Charts.

In 2009, it is my understanding that Steve Wynn, himself, came to see Garth to ask him to perform at the Wynn Hotel and Casino on the Los Vegas Strip. Wynn told him that he had full control over the concert and could do whatever he wanted. Wynn later said that he had to buy Garth a jet plane to seal the deal. Garth was to play one weekend a month, one show on Friday, two on Saturday, and one on Sunday and then fly back home for the rest of the month. And, because he had his own plane, the kids got to come along sometimes.

They tried it out for five weekends to see how it would work. Garth was able to play and still get back home to take care of his girls. Luckily for us, it worked out great and Garth agreed to a three-year contract. Almost immediately, the first year sold out. I think it was during the third year that my wife and I had the chance (because I'm on the mailing list for the Wynn and I received advanced notice of when he was playing) to see him in person. This was making up for missing him when he came to Salt Lake City in the Nineties.

It was a wonderful concert as I explained in the introduction. The Wynn web site shows that the last time Garth played was January 3 and 4, 2014, and I don't see anything planned for the future. All we can do is hope that Garth hasn't decided to really hang up his hat and retire for good this time. I hope to live to see him yet one more time. I would love to see the show he put on in the Nineties with the energy and the flying over the audience, but I suspect that that is gone forever. I hope, if you get a chance to see Garth, you'll jump at it. You won't be disappointed. Long live Garth Brooks.

# LEGACY OF GARTH BROOKS

In 1998, one in ten country records sold in this country was a Garth Brooks record.

He received the Award of Merit at the *29th Annual American Music Awards* in 2002. This recognizes people who have had "outstanding contributions to the musical entertainment of the American public."

Also, in 2002, he received *ASCAP's* Golden Note Award for outstanding contributions to American music.

And, also in 2002, he received a Hitmaker Award from the Songwriters Hall of Fame.

Garth was an official member of the San Diego Padres (1998-1999), the New York Mets (2000), and the Kansas City Royals (2005). He was a lousy ball player, but he loved every minute of it.

He was voted Entertainer of the Year by American Country Music six out of the ten years of the Nineties' decade: 1990, 1991, 1992, 1993, 1997, and 1998.

See the Awards section below for a list of his awards.

# AFTERWORD

Country music has always been very personal for me. I became acquainted with country music in the early Eighties when I met what was to be the best friend of my entire life. He was a disc jockey at a local country radio station. He loved rock and roll, but he loved country as well and convinced me that you could love both and not be weird.

Garth Brook's music is as personal as it gets. I think this is one reason he was (and is) as popular as he was. Almost every song has emotion and speaks to the heart. Many of them have been written as if he were singing just to me and I love him for that. This is what makes country music so good, to me.

I know Garth Brooks was not completely responsible, but I feel that he had a lot to do with country music moving in a more pop direction in the late Nineties. Shania Twain and Faith Hill were crossing over to the pop charts regularly and just last week, I listened to a "country" live show on TV and I could swear that most of it sounded like what is on the pop charts. We can thank (or curse, depending on your point of view) Garth Brooks for most of that.

You can contact me at http://www.number1project.com where I occasionally blog about things that interest me in the music world (mostly, the twentieth century). Go find it and read it and leave me a comment. I also have a Facebook fan page called "Legends of Rock & Roll". "Like" me and comment there, too. If you love the music as much as I do, you'll enjoy the trip. Thanks for reading.

I hope you have enjoyed this book as much as I have enjoyed writing it for you.

If you have liked what you read, will you please do me a favor and leave a review of "Garth Brooks". Thank you.

# AWARDS

2 Grammy Awards (total of 14 nominations)

17 American Music Awards (including "Artist of the '90s" won in 2000)

11 Country Music Association Awards

18 Academy of Country Music Awards

5 World Music Awards

10 People's Choice Awards

24 Billboard Music Awards

2 ASCAP Awards

2 Blockbuster Awards

Academy of Country Music Awards, Artist of the Decade (1990s)

Recording Industry Association of America, Artist of the Century (1900s)

1 Radio Music Award

2 Primetime Emmy Award nominations (Outstanding in a Variety of Music Program)

1 Golden Globe nomination (Best Original Song)

GLAAD Media Award for "We Shall Be Free"-1993

1 CMT Music Awards nomination, Collaborative Video of the Year for "Workin' For A Livin'" With Huey Lewis (2008)

Academy of Country Music Awards, inaugural "Crystal Milestone Award" honoring him as the top-selling country music artist in history, with album sales of over 128 million in the U.S. (2008)

2 American Music Awards Nominations (2008): Country Music – Favorite Male Artist Country Music – Favorite Album for "The Ultimate Hits"

# SELECTED DISCOGRAPHY

**Albums**

1989 - Garth Brooks (Capital Nashville)

1990 - No Fences (Capital Nashville)

1991 - Ropin' the Wind (Liberty Records)

1992 - The Chase (Liberty Records)

1993 - In Pieces (Liberty Records)

1995 - Fresh Horses (Liberty Records)

1997 - Sevens (Capital Nashville)

2001 - Scarecrow (Capital Nashville)

**As Chris Gaines**

1999 - Greatest Hits (Capital Records)

**Singles**

1989 - "Much Too Young (To Feel This Damn Old)"

1989 - "If Tomorrow Never Comes"

1990 - "Not Counting You"

1990 - "The Dance"

1990 - "Friends in Low Places"

1990 - "Unanswered Prayers"

1991 - "Two of a Kind, Workin' on a Full House"

1991 - "The Thunder Rolls"

1991 - "Rodeo"

1991 - "Shameless"

1991 - "What She's Doing Now"

1992 - "Papa Loved Mama"

1992 - "The River"

1992 - "We Shall Be Free"

1992 - "Somewhere Other Than the Night"

1993 - "Learning to Live Again"

1993 - "That Summer"

1993 - "Ain't Goin' Down ('Til the Sun Comes Up)"

1993 - "American Honky-Tonk Bar Association"

1993 - "Standing Outside the Fire"

1994 - "One Night a Day"

1994 - "Callin' Baton Rouge"

1995 - "She's Every Woman"

1995 - "The Fever"

1995 - "The Beaches of Cheyenne"

1996 - "The Change"

1996 - "It's Midnight Cinderella"

1996 - "That Ol' Wind"

1997 - "Longneck Bottle"

1998 - "She's Gonna Make It"

1998 - "Two Piña Coladas"

1998 - "To Make You Feel My Love"

1998 - "You Move Me"

1998 - "It's Your Song"

2000 - "Do What You Gotta Do"

2000 - "When You Come Back to Me Again"

2000 - "Wild Horses"

2001 - "Wrapped Up in You"

2002 - "Squeeze Me In" (with Trisha Yearwood)

2002 - "Thicker Than Blood"

2003 - "Why Ain't I Running"

2005 - "Good Ride Cowboy"

2006 - "Love Will Always Win" (with Trisha Yearwood)

2006 - "That Girl Is a Cowboy"

2007 - "More Than a Memory"

2007 - "Workin' for a Livin'" (with Huey Lewis)

2008 - "Midnight Sun"

# ABOUT THE AUTHOR

James Hoag has always been a big fan of Rock & Roll. Most people graduate from high school and then proceed to "grow up" and go on to more adult types of music. James got stuck at about age 18 and has been an avid fan of popular music ever since. His favorite music is from the Fifties, the origin of Rock & Roll and which was the era in which James grew up. But he likes almost all types of popular music including country music.

In 1980, he became friends with a man who introduced him to Country Music and he has been a strong fan of that genre of music ever since.

After working his entire life as a computer programmer, he is now retired and he decided to share his love of the music and of the performers by writing books that discuss the life and music of the various people who have meant so much to him over the years.

He calls each book a "love letter" to the stars that have enriched our lives so much. These people are truly Legends.

Made in the USA
Monee, IL
23 March 2021